wonderful world
Book series

YOU DON'T NEED A CAPE TO BE A HERO. YOU JUST NEED TO CARE.

Kid President

During the **Second World War,** Noor wanted to be a spy,

Second World War (1939 to 1945)
It was a big battle (fight) between two groups of countries - the 'Allies' and the 'Axis'. Many countries in the world were part of it.

So she was told she wasn't the right fit,

And that spies should be people with more **merit**.

Merit
Excellence; to be good at something

Dreamy and gentle, she wrote stories and songs,

And had very strict ideas about Right and Wrong.

So Noor trained hard,
without wasting a chance,

And was chosen to work as a spy in France.

She was the first female wireless operator,

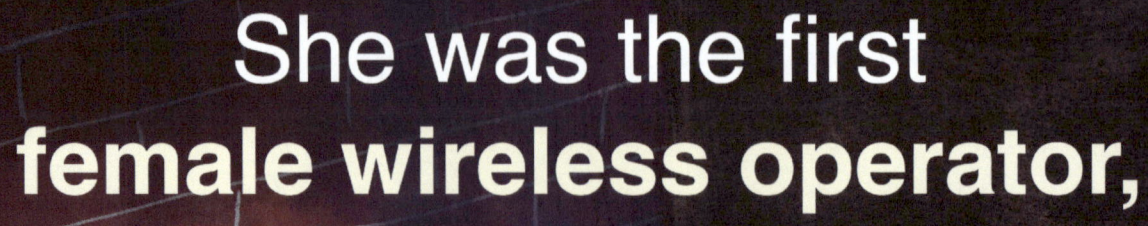

Wireless Operator
A person who operates a radio to send information over long distances

Radio
A device which sends and receives electric signals that can be heard through speakers as sound

Sent to get information which she'd radio later.

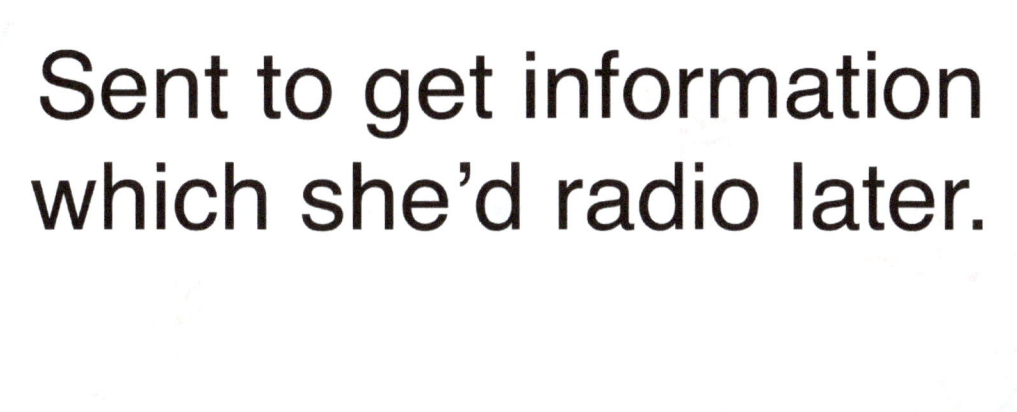

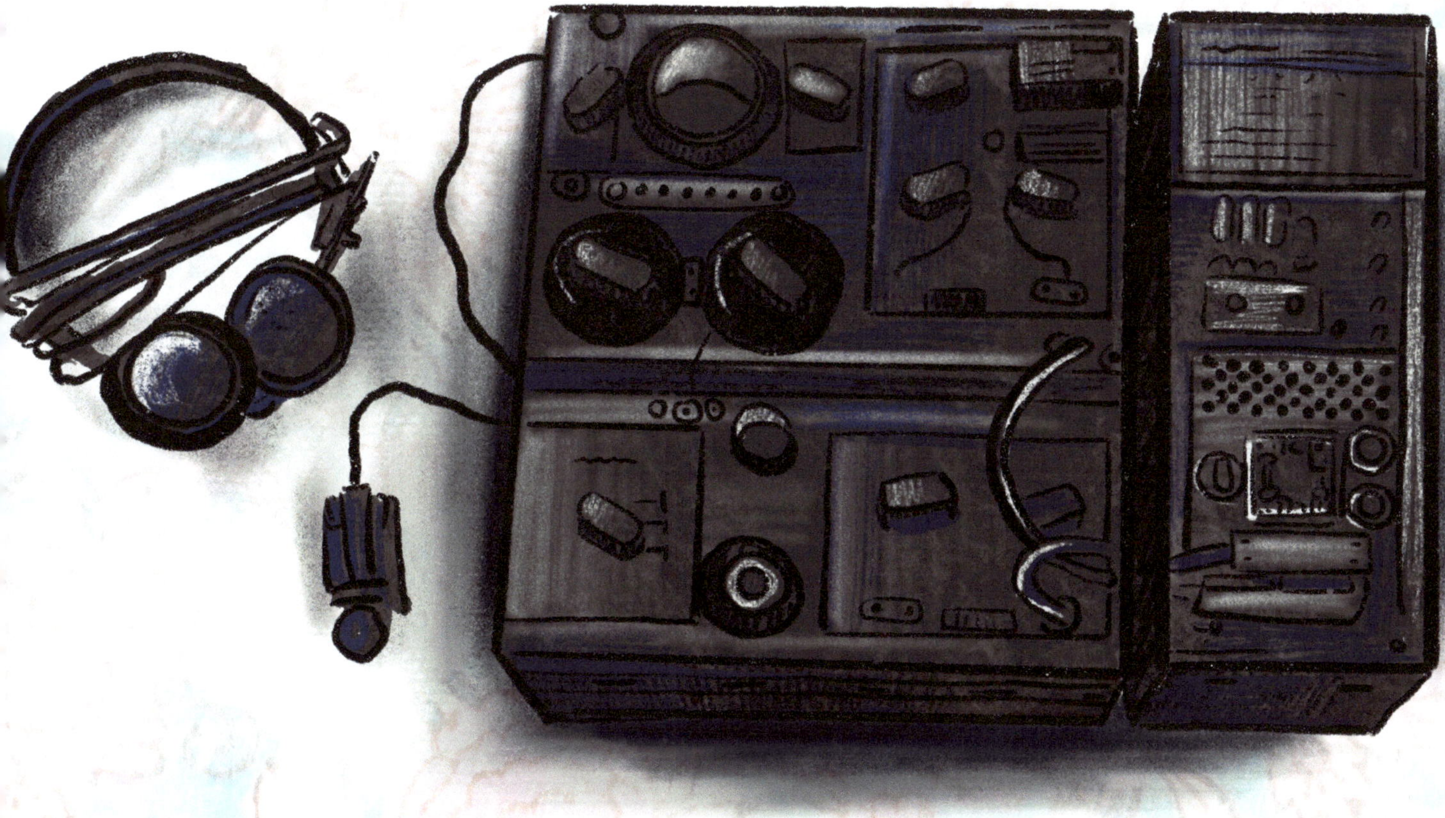

To stay safe, she kept moving from place to place,

So she'd pack up her things in a huge suitcase,

And disguise herself in different dresses and wigs.

But Noor didn't give up,
and did it the longest.

You can make this world a nicer place yet,

By choosing to be kind every chance you get.

Noor was **kind**, **creative**, and **courageous** too,

A wonderful person - just like you!

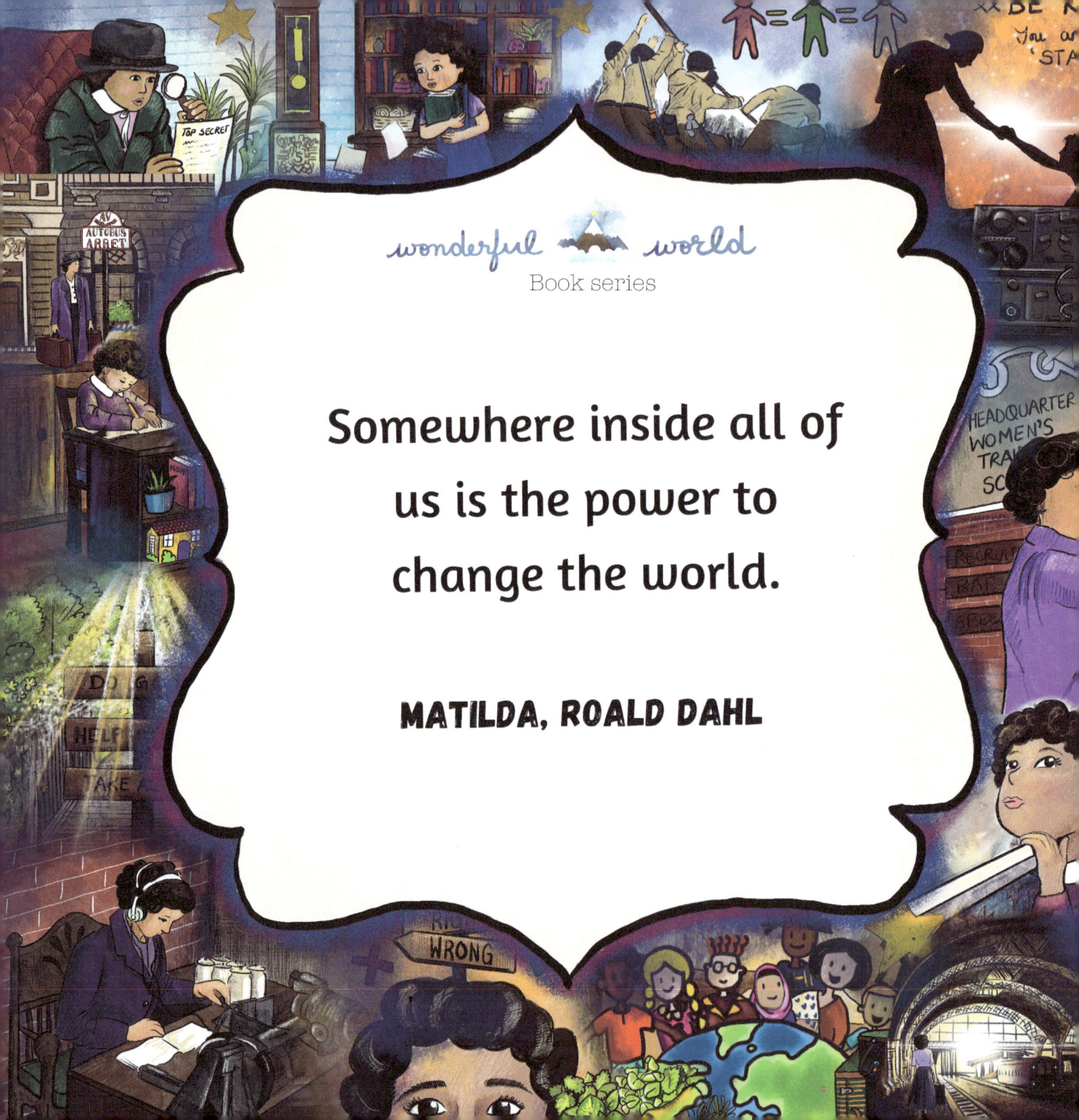

wonderful world
Book series

Somewhere inside all of us is the power to change the world.

MATILDA, ROALD DAHL

wonderful world
Book series

The Beginning

Thanks for reading my book.
I hope you've enjoyed it. For an independent author, ratings are very important for the success of their book. I'd be grateful if you could take a minute to rate this book on Amazon/ Goodreads.
Your support makes all the difference.

NOOR INAYAT KHAN

Timeline

1st January 1914
Noor was born in Moscow, to Hidayat Inayat Khan, a composer and Sufi teacher; and Khair-un-Nisa Inayat Khan. She was the eldest of four children.

1914
Shortly before the World War 1 started, they moved to Bloomsbury, London

1920
The family moved to Suresnes near Paris, France.

1927
Her father died, so 13-year-old Noor helped look after her siblings.

November 1940
Noor joined the Women's Auxiliary Air Force

June 1940
When France was conquered by Nazi Germany, the family fled to Britain.

1939
Noor studied child psychology and music. She loved to write. Her first book '20 Jataka Tales' was published.

February 1943
Noor began special training as a wireless operator in occupied territory, in Aylesbury.

17th June 1943
Noor was flown to Northern France, under the code-name Madeleine.

13th October 1943
Noor was arrested. It was later revealed that she refused to give any information, even under torture.

13th September 1944
Noor was executed at Dachau Concentration Camp, and she died shouting 'Liberté' (liberty).

HELLO

Thank you for reading my book! I was very excited to write Noor's story because it's so inspiring and beautiful. She was a pacifist because of her religious beliefs (Sufi Muslim), and opposed to violence of any sort. However, during the Second World War, she felt it was wrong to stay neutral. So, she enlisted, but requested that she not be put in a position where she'd be responsible for the death of another person. This meant occupying the most dangerous posts, and putting her own life at risk.

Her story drew me, because she was described as very nervous, clumsy, quiet, and very shy. Her superiors, after the interview, commented that she was not 'overburdened with brains'. (Patriarchy/Racism/Sexism much, maybe?)

Nevertheless, she was the first female wireless operator sent to France from Britain during the Second World War, and she was MARVELLOUS. Few people lasted in that role for more than few weeks, because they were caught and executed. She lasted five whole months, and because she kept disguising and changing place every day, hiding wires in clotheslines, hiding her equipment in a bundle of twigs etc. Even when she was caught, it was only because she was betrayed. But this woman, labelled inept and inadequate, did what no one else could.

Unfortunately, she was caught and tortured for information but she gave nothing away. And when executed, she died shouting 'Liberty'.

I think her story is one which deserves to be told more commonly. Of course, since my readers are very little kids, I've left out the most tragic part, and focused on her incredible idealism and courage.

Though sad, reading of people like this fills me with such hope. If we are part of a world which produces people like this, surely there's hope for humanity. Don't you agree?

Love, R Julian

Check out
www.ramyajulian.com/picturebooks

Glossary

Second World War (1939 to 1945)
It was a big battle (fight) between two groups of countries - the 'Allies' and the 'Axis'. Many countries in the world were involved.

Allies
A group of countries who fought the Axis powers in the World War II, including the United Kingdom, USA, and Soviet Union.

Axis Powers
A group of countries who fought the Allied Powers/ Allies in World War II, including Germany, Italy, and Japan.

Nazis
A group of people who believed that anyone who looks different, speaks different, thinks different, or acts different from them should be fought. They wanted to have complete power over everyone.
(Author's note: I know this is not exact, but as a mother of young kids, I feel a more technically correct definition would be suitable for older readers.)

Spy
A person who keeps secret watch on another person or a thing to get information.

Glossary

Merit
Excellence; to be good at something.

Non violence
Against fighting; avoiding anything that could hurt or harm others.

Equipment
A set of tools needed to do a particular job.

Information
Knowledge or facts.

Wireless Operator
A person who operates a radio to send information over long distances.

Radio
A device which sends and receives electric signals that can be heard through speakers as sound.

Secret Code

Fill in the alphabets corresponding to the numbers in the code to reveal the secret message.

A	B	C	D	E	F	G	H	I	J
1	2	3	4	5	6	7	8	9	10

K	L	M	N	O	P	Q	R	S	T
11	12	13	14	15	16	17	18	19	20

U	V	W	X	Y	Z
21	22	23	24	25	26

Message for you:

25	15	21

1	18	5

1	23	5	19	15	13	5

wonderful world

Book series

About the Author

Author, illustrator, and dentist, **Ramya Julian** finished her first novel at the age of ten and she avers it was very well received though it was read only by her brother.

She has all the hobbies of a maiden Victorian aunt – reading, writing, painting, crocheting, knitting and sewing, and the temperament of one. When she's not guilt-tripping her two daughters into good behaviour, she can be found devouring books, crafting poems and puns, and chuckling at her own witticisms. She grew up in India and now lives with her husband and their two daughters in London.

She has experienced so much joy through the enchanting artistry of many authors and creators, that she aspires to share at least some of it through her writing.

To see more of her work, visit **www.ramyajulian.com**

www.ramyajulian.com

Also in this series

NEXT IN LINE: MANY MANY MORE WONDERFUL DIVERSE HEROES

TO MY NEWSLETTER
For the latest news and free printables
www.ramyajulian.com

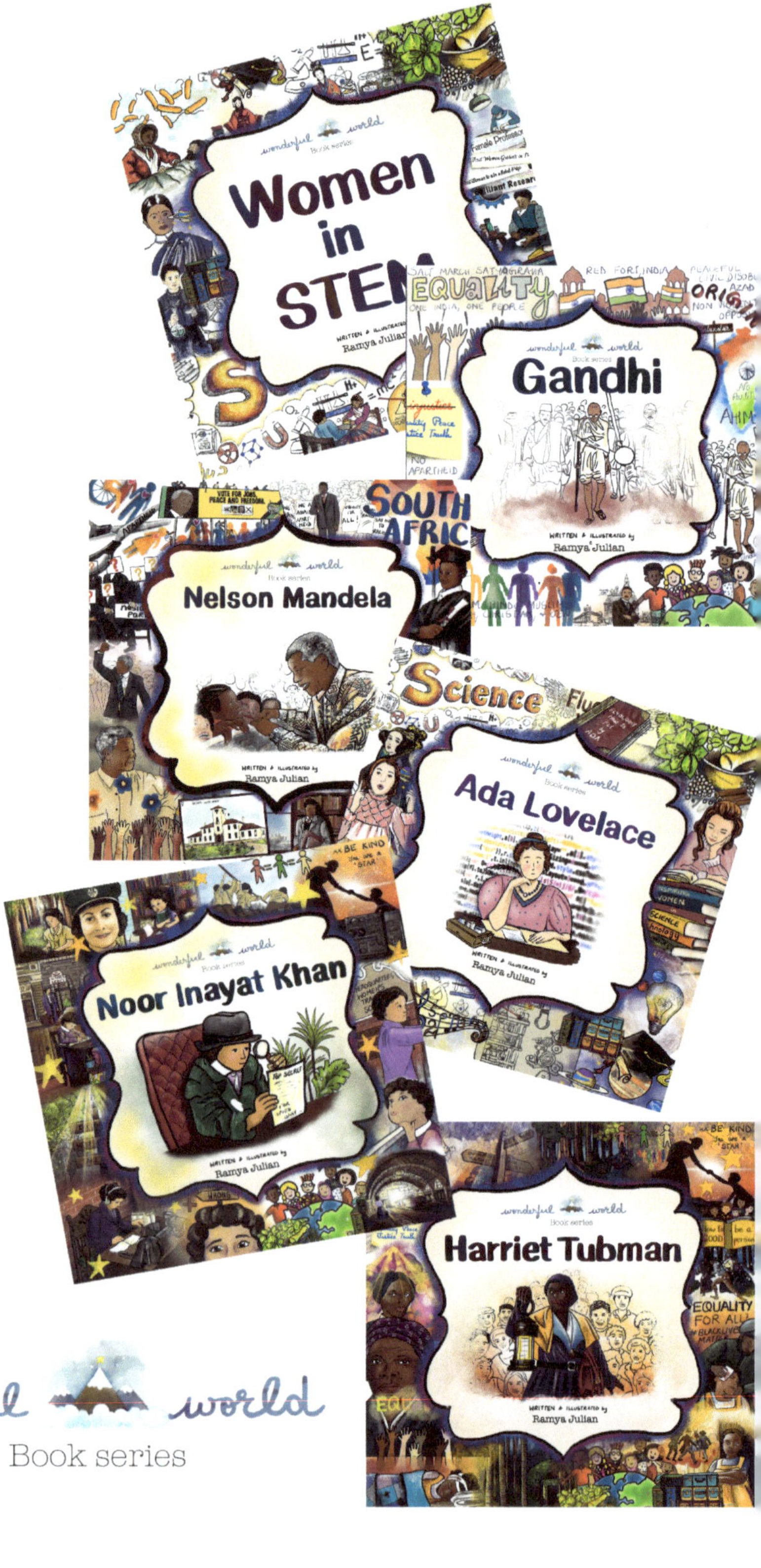

@RAMYAJULIAN

wonderful world
Book series